Poetry Tr
Pass

Compiled ana Edited by
Kaye Lynne Booth And Robbie
Cheadle

This anthology may contain previously or simultaneously published materials.

Introduction by Kaye Lynne Booth

Compiled and edited by Kaye Lynne Booth and Roberta Eaton Cheadle.

Cover design by Teagan R. Genevieve

Notice: This anthology contains both American and British spellings, dependent upon the country of origin of the poet.

Table of Contents

Introduction

I remember the unit on Haiku in the fourth grade, where we not only read, but were also tasked with writing this beautiful form of poetry. As a young girl, I was in awe of such an expressive form of writing. You see, in order to express what you wanted to say in the correct number and placement of syllables, you had to make every word count, with this syllabic form of poetry. You had to be very particular in your word choices, using descriptive words which brought certain imagery to mind. And when you put each line together in the proper order, with the perfect words to convey your message, and it all comes together to create a vision in the reader's mind, it was like magic; the kind of magic which allows one to see the world in a whole new way. During that nine-week unit on Haiku, my eyes were opened to a beauty I had never known before. And then, my class went on to study proper letter writing, because when I was a kid, there was no email and letter writing was still very much a thing to learn. And there were other assignments which left no time for practicing the writing of Haiku, and it wasn't long until I didn't think about it anymore. But I never forgot that beauty, or the feelings that it stirred in a nine-year-old girl.

And that's why I was so pleased to host Robbie Cheadle's "Treasuring Poetry" blog series on my blog site, *Writing to be Read*. Because poetry has had a special place in my heart ever since. And why *WordCrafter Press* publishes a *Poetry Treasures* anthology each year. It's my way to pay tribute to all of the beautiful forms of poetry, and to the poets who craft them.

This year's theme is Passions. Robbie chose it, but I thought it a fitting theme for such an emotional and expressive form of writing. Passions explode onto the page in vibrant colors, and soothe the soul in cool pastels. Sometimes they appear in earth tones, but never in boring old black and white, or monotone.

The poems contained within this volume speak to all that is passionate within us, the passions which drive us, and some of the many passions which drive us. The poetry and artworks within these pages are unique to their creators, and many of the passions they express, we can relate well to.

I hope you will join us now as we journey with thirteen individual poets, delving into their own passions and the passions of humanity.

January guest - Robbie Cheadle

My January poet was intended to be Walt Page. Walt was unable to participate as he was unwell at the time. Sadly, Walt passed a few months later. I miss his beautiful love poetry.

About Robbie Cheadle

Award-winning, bestselling author, Robbie Cheadle, has published thirteen children's book and three poetry books. Her work has also appeared in poetry and short story anthologies.

Robbie also has two novels published under the name of Roberta Eaton Cheadle and has horror, paranormal, and fantasy short stories featured in several anthologies under this name.

The ten Sir Chocolate children's picture books, co-authored by Robbie and Michael Cheadle, are written in sweet, short rhymes which are easy for young children to follow and are illustrated with pictures of delicious cakes and cake decorations. Each book also includes simple recipes or biscuit art directions which children can make under adult supervision.

Robbie's blog includes recipes, fondant and cake artwork, poetry, and book reviews. https://robbiesinspiration.wordpress.com/

Words for my son

Words flow fluidly from my mind to pen,
they come very easily to me
So why is it when I speak to you,
I just cannot seem to make you see
That I love you, my most special boy,
I am your number one fan
It is a joyous journey to watch you,
becoming an extraordinary man.
You have an amazing mind,
you're like an adult when we engage
It makes it hard to understand the teenage angst
that within you must rage,
You make us smile when you sit laughing
at some amusing situation in a book
Although I can get really cross
when you give me your uncooperative look.
My own teenage years a distant memory
but I do remember
The emotional highs and lows,
like violent thunderstorms during December
An adventurous and exploratory time in your life,
bursting with so much possibility
To take advantage, you need to control body and mind
and take responsibility
You are exceptionally empathetic and kind,
you always give to others
I take delight when I see you treating everyone
as your sisters and brothers.
Words for my son is included in *Open a new door, a collection of poems
by Kim Blades and*

Robbie Cheadle.

A Selection of Haiku

Have you been to hell?
Manifests differently
Furtive shape shifter

***

Burning, deprived lungs
Grasp life-giving oxygen
Too little, too late

***

From cold ashes
Of heartless devastation
A phoenix rises

***

Beneath chalky white
Skin, transparent with illness
Blue veins pulse weakly

***

When loved ones sicken
We transfer our life essence
From ourselves to them

About these haiku

These poems are all about illness by various members of my family over
the past 20 years. Both my sons were born with chronic illnesses, and

they have undergone 40 operations between them. My father has had three serious illnesses when he has come close to losing his life, my mother is a breast cancer survivor, and most recently, my husband has been ill with encephalitis (a bacterial illness that causes inflammation of the brain).

These haiku are an expression of my feelings during these times of emotional turmoil and distress.

No Tears, a Tanka poem

I never shed tears
When I learned of her passing
I didn't understand
I've kept my unvented grief
Tightly wrapped up inside me

About No Tears

My Granny Joan died when I was 11 years old. I didn't really understand death at that time, even though I had already read books like Salem's Lot and The Stand, both by Stephen King. I didn't realise the permanence of my loss.

During a road trip in January 2022, I visited George in the Western Cape. This was the town where my Granny Joan lived out her last years and died. I lived in George for two years when I was 10 and 11. I tried to find her grave. There were three graveyards, and I wasn't sure which was the right one. I managed to track it down on the internet, but sadly it was locked when we visited. The office that had the key was closed as it was the week after New Year. South Africa, as a rule, only starts back at work during the second week of January each year.

My mother said I am a romantic and shouldn't mind not seeing Granny's grave. But I did mind. I wanted to lay flowers on her grave to let her know I remember her.

Peacock Romance

Dowdy and plain in brown
She stands and watches
Her prospective mate as he crosses the lawn
Blissfully unaware
Of her thoughtful stare

Picture credit: photograph of a peahen by Robbie Cheadle

He cuts a fine figure
Resplendent in blue
This despite his splendid tail dragging behind
Glancing up, he spots her,
It's love at first sight

Picture credit: photograph of a peacock by Robbie Cheadle

In a show of interest
She descends the stairs
Passion ignited; his tail spreads out fanlike
Overwhelmed, he takes off
With her in pursuit

Picture credit: photograph of a peacock by Robbie Cheadle

Picture credit: Peacocks at Champagne Caste Hotel in the Drakensberg by Robbie Cheadle
Romance of the Peacocks is included in *Lion Scream, Syllabic Poetry About Southern African Wildlife* by Robbie Cheadle.

Bold Lover, a 99-syllable poem

One sleepy eye opens
Encounters shy dark
Reaches out with tentative fiery caress
Lover shrinks from his touch
Rosy blush ensues

***

Emboldened he rises
Pink quickly dissolves
Burnished gold splendour announcing his hot love
Tremulous withdrawal
By passion's object

***

Clear lust overwhelms her
Fleet footed she runs
An ethereal figure in a black gown
Giving chase is futile
She's slipped away

Bold Lover is included in *Lion Scream, Syllabic Poetry About Southern African Wildlife* by
Robbie Cheadle.

Inspiration for Bold Lover: Picture taken in the Madikwe Game Reserve by Robbie Cheadle

One for me, None for you

A mammoth structure
It dominates the rise
A tribute to corruption
Ill gotten gains and lies
Luxurious cars gleam
A dozen – or more
Fast and sleek, they hint
At what is in store
Adorned with art
A magnificent hall
Ornate vases and statues
Loom up – proud and tall
Tea and cake is served
Cups plated with gold
A multitude of servants
Uniforms bright and bold
A story begins to unfold
Told with arrogance and pride
A tale of self enrichment -
The listeners beguiled
The audience like insects
Trapped in a golden lair
The flow of silky words
Attempts minds to ensnare
At last – the flow dwindles
This self endulgent river
The opportunity is taken
To escape – with a shiver
On route back home
Time to sit and reflect

Youthful beggars flash by
Their budding lives wrecked
The gluttenous excesses
Left further behind
The contrast so stark
Its seems almost designed
Southern Africa we pray
For a future that's bright
We cannot afford
To give up this fight

About One for you, None for me

This poem holds a lot of meaning for me. I wrote it after visiting the home of a couple who had enriched themselves through the excessive corruption and self-enrichment that is so prevalent in Southern African countries. Written in rhyming verse, before I was aware that rhyming verse is no longer in favour with poets, it conveys my frustration about the growing poverty gap that exists in many southern African countries and the misappropriation of funds meant for education, healthcare, and other upliftment programmes for the common people.

This poem is included in *Open a new door, a collection of poems by Kim Blades and*
Robbie Cheadle.

The Pet, a 99-syllable poem

Beyond the doorway lies
Beloved animal
Eyes laughing, he smiles with doggy affection
Watching my every move
with rapt attention
Whimpering with pleasure
As I draw closer
He runs up to me: Is a walk on offer?
How could I not react
With equal delight?
Through the streets of the town
We walk, side-by-side
But at the wood he throws decorum aside
Like a dervish, he's gone
But soon he'll be back

Picture credit: Original fondant artwork by Robbie Cheadle

February guest - Smitha Vishwanath

About Smitha Vishwanath

Smitha Vishwanath is your quintessential 'bored banker' turned writer. After a rewarding career in Banking in the Middle East where she worked for leading banks in senior positions, she quit and moved to India in July 2018 with her husband who had been transferred to the country on an international assignment. Thereon she began her writing journey.

'Roads' is the first book she has co-authored. Having lived and studied in different countries and different states within India and worked with different cultures, Smitha understands that 'change' and 'ups and downs' are very much a part of life. It is this experience that reflects in her poems and her writing which are filled with positivity, acceptance and willingness to change for the better.

She also writes regularly through her blog: **https://lifeateacher.wordpress.com**[1]

Two little birdies

Two little birdies
In a sand pit
Fight over a titbit
Under the trees.
Two little birdies
I see them fly
with the wind
in the blue sky.
I watch longingly
from my seat
and wish, I, too, could be just as free
and fly with the breeze, where I please.
Two little birdies
perch upon my windowsill
I wonder what brings them back
And I overhear birdie number 1, say,
'Look, she's warm inside, yet
it is us she envies.'
These earthlings keep happiness at bay
forgetting to make the most of each new day.'
'How sad that human greed hath no end
They forget they must transcend
Petty hurdles and troubles along the way,'
birdie number two replied solemnly,
Teaching me a lesson or two that day
before they flew away.
A lesson so simple, yet so profound-
happiness is within, not a thing not to be found.

Picture credit: Pexels – photo by ian – two little birds

A child called, 'Passion'

A child called, Passion,
I met him on my walk, one day
and asked him to come home.
He replied, 'On one condition-
only if you give me your undivided attention.'
'How difficult could that be? aloud, I wondered,
I raised a family with children- two!'
Smiling impishly, he said 'Not much, if you surrendered."
I laughed at his presumptuousness
Little knowing how true to his words he'd be.
The moment, Passion, walked in through my door
He obscured the rest of the world from sight
and kept me waking into the night
He pranced around all day-tireless, and unbound.
It made me loathe the day, him, I found.
Passion was a stubborn child
demanding complete allegiance.
His appetite was unappeased,
his thirst unquenched;
he made no allowance!
A ruthless master, a sorcerer
He turned me into a willing slave.
I fulfilled his every bidding;
the years went by, I couldn't tell
and the children flew before I knew.
But, Passion, he stayed behind.
I grew old, and he grew kind.
Passion, that stubborn child
remained wilful until the end
and refused to leave,

even though my body was hard to mend.
He nourished my body and fed my soul
And made me feel as good as whole.
Passion, that stubborn child, simply would not let go;
no doctor could understand that child's miraculous cure.
So, if you ever cross paths with a child called, 'Passion.'
Hold onto him with a firm hand
Even if you must endure.
Lug around for a while if you must-
but don't ever let go.
For when all the others leave-
He will be standing by your side
For, Passion, is a stubborn child
and loyal as can be
Let nobody tell you otherwise.

Picture credit: Vase of flowers painted and photographed by Smitha V

Zachem

Dying children standing in deep snow-
a 'Z' formation
What does it mean?
Zachem?
In Russian, means, 'for what?'
When everyone is second guessing; so must I-
'Z' is for zoo; where animals are caged
'Z' is for zealot; an oppressor
'Z' is for zip; used for restricting access
'Z' is for zen; living in harmony with the universe
'Z' is for zealous; passionate for a cause; I wonder, even to die?
'Z' is the last alphabet, the end!
'Z' is for zany; bizarre or comical
'Z' stands for Zapad, meaning 'West'; where the sun sets,
and 'Z' stands for Za Pobedy, meaning victory; I wonder, over what?
Since nobody knows what 'Z' stands for
Would it be overly optimistic of me
to think it symbolizes, 'Peace'?
Peace between two ideologies- communism and capitalism
Moving parallel like railway tracks
Never to meet. Except as in '**Z**'.

The above poem and picture is based on the news dated 07032022-
https://nypost.com/2022/03/07/terminally-ill-kids-form-z-in-snow-
for-russian-propaganda/

The gift

Eighteen green stones
One for every two years' gone
Embedded in a cast of gold
Strung together in an unbreakable bond.
Built on sweet mango pickle, Toblerone
And dwindling memories of life at eleven
I wear our friendship around my neck
A past salvaged by your patience and time.
I trace my fingers on each lemony drop
That gently rests on my chest and falls below my collarbone
And I see a celebration of who you've become
From a pig-tailed girl to a woman, who found her passion, in creation.
You could've given me anything
but you chose to give me this:
a gift made by you
Especially for me
And I see you haven't changed- you're the same
Beautiful, sensitive and creative
And the memories flood back
of lamington cakes, tamarind trees and the year five dormitory.

Picture credit: Pexels photograph by Sebastian Arie Voortman

If I could gift you anything

If I could gift you anything, I would give *you*
a gift worthy of you;
one that I would want for me too!
I would give you a cloud to float your troubles away,
and shower you with peace to last all day.
I would give you a rainbow, bright and cheerful to tread on
and a box of the choicest blessings for every dawn.
I would give you a map to end your confusion
and a compass to reach your destination
I would give you an elixir to good h*ealth*
and the magic potion to find your *true wealth*.
If I could gift you anything, I would give *you*
A gift that I would want for me too-
The key to your passion
and to fulfil it, a never-ending determination.

Picture credit: Pexels-pixabay-If I had to gift you

One last time

If this be the last day
Darling, let's dine and dance-
One last time
And let's hold hands and pray
To be together in the other world
And if there be such a thing as 'Rebirth'
Then may we meet again.
One life with you isn't enough
Nor seven would be; I had it easy
I've gotten lazy
Let's skype the children
I want to look at them

Until I no longer can
I want to feel pride
One last time.
I'd like to thank Him
For the good life,
For family, for love, for my sister-
If only we had more time together,
I'll tell Him for the last time
That He wrote the perfect story
And if ever there is an 'Again'
He could simply rewind and replay mine
Bring me back under the same sun-sign
and keep everything else the same
There's nothing more I can think of-
that I'd want to do or say
I'll close my eyes with not an ounce of regret
but with a hope and a prayer
that I'd come back wiser the next time around-
so I could gulp down every sorrow
knowing there's a better 'morrow
And, sip every joy, sweet and slow,
like the largo, if this be the last day.

Picture credit: Pexels by Leeloo the First

March guest – Abbie Taylor

About Abbie Taylor

Abbie Johnson Taylor is the author of three novels, two poetry collections and a memoir. Her work has appeared in The Weekly Avocet, The Writer's Grapevine, and Magnets and Ladders. She's visually impaired and lives in Sheridan, Wyoming, where for six years, she cared for her totally blind late husband who became partially paralyzed as a result of a stroke soon after they were married. With a BA in music, she has worked as a registered music therapist with nursing home residents, facilitated a support group for visually impaired adults, taught Braille, and served on the advisory board to a trust fund providing adaptive equipment and services to the blind and visually impaired. Please visit her website at: https://www.abbiejohnsontaylor.com

Condiments

Garlic salt, black pepper, chili powder,
I used under his direction after his paralyzing strokes.
Having loved to cook,
he wanted me to prepare homemade meals,
not just pop something frozen into the oven.
For six years, I cooked his meals,
wouldn't have blamed him if he'd walked out on me
in search of a better cook.
He always complimented me on my cooking,
his arm encircling my waist,
kiss soft against my cheek.
Now that he's left this world,
condiments sit in the cupboard, rarely used.

The Black Hole

A Shakespearean actor with an evocative voice,
Dad needed to speak,
but words wouldn't come.
For years, he struggled, stammering, swearing,
to wrestle beloved language from his stroke's black hole,
often succeeding until the end
when no more words emerged.

The Music Lady

I approached your bed, took your hand,
introduced myself, offered to share my passion for music.
Bringing relief from boredom, pain, paralysis,
an alternative to television,
I sat beside you, picked up my guitar,
strummed a chord or two, started singing.
I asked if you had a favorite song,
sang it just for you.
Your family came—they liked my music.
In your last days, I often held your hand,
sang hymns and other songs you liked.
My touch and voice comforted you.
Your family asked me to sing your favorite song
as your casket was carried out.
They told me how much
my joyful and comforting music meant to you.

April guest - Chris Hall

About Chris Hall

Chris describes herself as a compulsive story-teller, cat slave and hen keeper. Originally from the UK, she now resides in the Western Cape of South Africa.

Her most recent novels, 'Song of the Sea Goddess' and its sequel, 'Spirit of the Shell Man' were inspired by the charm and beauty of her adopted country where, in Chris's vivid imagination, myth and reality collide on the southern shores of Africa.

Other novels:

'You'll Never Walk Alone - Thrills and Spills in 1980s Liverpool'

'Following the Green Rabbit - a fantastical adventure'

'The Silver Locket' (published under pen name, Holly Atkins)

'Song of the Sea Goddess', 'Spirit of the Shell Man' and 'Following the Green Rabbit' are also available as audiobooks.

A selection of her poetry is included in 'Creation and the Cosmos - a poetic anthology', published by Raw Earth Ink in 2021.

She has also published a tiny taster of her work in a short story collection, 'A Sextet of Shorts'.

More of her short fiction has appeared in 'Adler's Writing' and 'One Minute Wit'. Her work also appears in the 'Writing My City' anthology, published in Cape Town in 2019.

Visit Chris's website at https://lunas-online.com/ to read her short fiction, fan fiction, mini-series, poetry and more.

Home for the holidays

Flying north, homeward bound?
to the bright lights of the well-kept city
to snow-bound circles, pools of light in the darkness
shining from sturdy houses onto well-lit streets
where ice sparkles on windows and children
exhale frosty breath while
making snow angels
on white-carpeted lawns.
But my heart remains
where summer's sun bakes the thirsty earth
on the opposing hemisphere
where barefoot children dance on dusty paths
and goats and cattle roam on the edge of pitted highways
here, where the African moon reclines on her back
for this is now
my home.

Juxtaposition

Luxury cars displayed, glass-encased,
a stone's throw from where
people make their homes
under flyovers.
Leafy suburbs, all high walls and gated communities,
where the fat pony's stable
is a step up
from the best built shack.
Assuage your guilt by paying someone
to mow your lawn
or clean your house
for a cut above the minimum wage.
Turn your head away, un-see them all;
the beggar by the robot,
the thin woman with the baby on her back
picking through the trash.
Don't look back
Don't glance over your shoulder.
It's all still there.
High up, in your shiny city apartment overlooking the city-bright
lights
you forget the people
shivering on the street.

Enigma of Giza

What secrets lie behind those sightless eyes?
What words remain unspoken by those muted lips?
Splendid in your solitude, presiding over barren sands
Relic of antiquity made inscrutable by time.
Awed, we gaze upon your enigmatic face
Charmed by the essence of your fading gaze
Veiled in ancient mystery, emblem of eternity
Focused on a future which persists beyond our ken.
Come, rise phoenix-like from that aeolian tomb!
Ascend the dunes and navigate the silken sands of yore
Spirit traversing the tracks of vanished acolytes
A wild wind whispering the secrets of the past.

Death or Glory

Hiding in barns and outbuildings by day
Walking in hedgerows undercover of night
Head down, senses alert
Day after day, avoiding the light.
The border's not far; check point ahead
Dive for cover or put up a fight?
Crouch in the undergrowth; senses strain
The longest day; freedom's in sight.
Evening comes, it's time to run
Pound across fields, vault over gates
Soldiers shout, shots are fired
Adrenaline pumps, heart thumps.
Hounds at my heels, boots thud on the ground
Screw up my courage, don't ever look back
It's now or never, my ultimate hope
Striving for freedom, just one final leap.

The Lightning Tree

We called it the lightning tree. Stunted and blackened it stood resolute, stark against the moon-bright night, while shooting stars circled wildly over the soft, velvet plain. Here we farmed, here cattle roamed over long-stemmed grass and here we were happy.

but drought-stricken land
thirsted for seven summers:
grass withered, we fled.

The lightning tree still stands, its final branch fallen, the stars the only witnesses. Finally, the rains return, falling softly, pattering on the parched land, washing over sun-bleached rocks and the desolate dried-up plain.

the ground drinks deeply
yellow and pink flowers bloom
but no-one will see.

The lightning tree still stands, but no-one sees but the stars.

The Last of His Kind

He was the last of his kind.
Wearily he lay down,
waiting for the end.
He'd sensed it coming.
The heavens darkened,
flames filled the sky.
The celestial destructor bore down
upon his Mother Earth.
Would she survive?
Would others come after?
No answer came.
His body crisped to dust.

What will become of us?

She
at one time
could have held
the whole world in her hands.
The wide oceans and the high mountains,
the hills, the valleys and the lakes;
the mighty forests
and sweetly painted flowers;
she encompassed all of her bounty.
The beasts both wild and gentle roamed
across all the fertile earth, free and fruitful.
It was paradise.
But then Sons of Adam and Daughters of Eve were unleashed.
They grew wise and strong; their numbers swelled. They spread.
And as their knowledge grew, so did their ambition.
Their need to abuse, oppress and exploit.
She slapped them down like the wicked children they were.
She sent earthquakes and tidal waves; war, famine and disease.
But still they persisted.
She tries to cling on, keeping it together for the good of the world.
But the children of the world press harder, mine deeper, defile and
destroy.
And when she can no longer hold on to us?
What then?
What will
become
of us?

May guest – Yvette M. Calleiro

About Yvette M. Calleiro

Yvette M. Calleiro is the author of the Chronicles of the Diasodz fantasy series, HYPE, and several short stories. As a heavily addicted reader of both young adult and adult novels, she spends most of her time pseudo-living in paranormal worlds with her fictional friends (and boyfriends).

When she's living among real people, she is a middle school Reading and Language Arts teacher. She's been sharing her love of literature with her students for over twenty years. Besides writing about the various characters that whisper (and sometimes scream) in her head, she enjoys traveling, watching movies, spending quality time with family and friends, and enjoying the beauty of the ocean.

Yvette lives in Miami, Florida, with her incredible son who has embraced her love for paranormal and adventurous stories. She also shares her space with an assortment of crazy saltwater animals in her 300-gallon tank.

Be in the Moment

BE
Such a tiny little word.
If you look too quickly,
You might miss it.
But, oh, what power it has!
Its life-sustaining energy
Stills chaos in an instant.
IN just being,
Allow your breath to calm the mind.
Slow down.
Breathe in.
Breathe out.
Notice.
Feel.
Let go.
THE beauty of life
Begins and ends with one breath.
Still the worries, anxieties, and negative thoughts.
Awaken your senses.
Feel the earth beneath you,
The wind caressing your hair,
The sun warming your skin.
Hear the birds serenading the world,
The laughter of a child,
The rustle of the trees' leaves.
Smell the sea salt as waves crash upon the shore,
The freshly cut lawn on a dewy morning,
The percolating coffee.
See the puffy, white clouds as they lazily stroll by,
The precious poodle pulling excitedly on his chain

On his quest to mark a new territory,
The elderly woman tenderly caring for her roses.
MOMENT by moment,
Pause, breathe, and cherish
The precious life you are given.
Just be.
Be in the moment.

Ocean's Calm

Ebb and flow,
Come and go,
Nothing stays the same.
The writing in the sand
Dissipates with no resistance,
Welcoming the opportunity to
Transform into newness once again.
Every grain has its story.
Left alone, it is carried away,
Coerced to move at the ocean's will.
No control of its destiny,
But collectively, a strength is grown.
The concentration compounds its essence
To become firm
But not rigid.
Ocean waters flow over and through,
At times angrily pounding and crashing,
But the sand sighs and
Smooths away the intrusion.
Knowing it is safe to enjoy the waves.
Come and go,
Ebb and flow.

In the Depths Below

Sparkling diamonds glitter upon the surface
And beckon me to come play.
Sand sifts between my toes,
Grounding me
But not for long.
Small waves lap against the shore
And draw me in
As they pull away.
I give in to the urge,
Don my gear and wade into the salty water
Until I can no longer stand.
Heart races,
Anticipation and excitement
Course through my veins.
Respirator in mouth,
I become one with the ocean
And dive
Deeper and deeper,
Allowing the water to hug me tightly
In her cool embrace.
I inhale air and release bubbles.
Inhale
Exhale
Inhale
Exhale
My heart slows
Into a rhythmic, meditative state
Only the sea can give me.
The ocean comes alive before my eyes.
Brilliant blues, vibrant yellows

Swim around me,
Curious and skittish.
Corals sway with the water's rhythm.
I drift,
Still and silent,
Except for my breaths,
Surrounded by life and beauty,
Quiet and calm.
My gauge says I must ascend.
I sigh and say goodbye
To my underwater friends
And vow to return again
To my home away from home,
The depths of the sea.

To the Depths Below (an Etheree)

diamonds glitter upon the sea's surface
she beckons me to join her and play
heart races as I acquiesce
with gear in place, I dive deep
breathing becomes rhythmic
peace envelopes me
bright fish swim past
curious
playful
free

A Story is Born (Butterfly Cinquain)

my muse
seduces me
write for me, he whispers
his words softly caress and tease
I sigh
my mind and hands are his to use
supple, eager to please
his creation
written

Claimed (Nonet)

his fingers linger on my soft skin
caress all my imperfections
his lips travel down my neck
my body liquifies
strong arms pull me close
sigh escapes me
heated breath
whispers
mine

June guest – Willow Willers

About Willow Willers

Willow Willers, lives in southern England with her husband and their beloved, retired, guide dog Ruby. Willow is the mother of three boys, all now grown and flown to live their own lives. Luckily, they do keep in touch and visit often. There is now a daughter in law and two beautiful grandsons.

Willow started writing when she was very young but a serious accident twenty odd years ago made her re-evaluate her life. Learning to walk again does that and she started writing again.

Writing poetry and prose has helped Willow a great deal. In fact, she thinks it has saved her life.

Willow shares here beautiful poetry on her blog here: https://willowdot21.wordpress.com

Passion

It bubbles and it rises
Festering it multiplies
Takes over and it rules
Turning us all into fools
It wants us to devour
Taking our souls to deflower
Robbing us of the power to say no
As we surrender and let go.
Soon it becomes an obsession
Between ecstasy and depression
Be it for sex, food, money or fashion
There's nothing quite like passion

Passion, A Decima

You and I, an eclectic blend
Take our essence inhale and sip
Your fingers make my senses flip
Gently arouse my desires I bend
To your will, I crave the end
Erotic juices running free
Lips cup places they shouldn't be
Every inch of our bodies steam
Climaxing as one we both scream
Bodies electric, our souls free

Passion, A Tanka

True passion for life
consumes just like a fire
urging the senses
to devour and embrace
lust for the definition

The Sea

I have a passion for the sea
Gentle motion and sound set me free
To catch a wave and ride it high
Through water funnels to the sky
Aqua cathedrals where I long to be
I have a passion for the sea

Passion, A Haiku

You reach out, touch me
an electric ecstasy
ignites our passion

Academic Passion

Figures were his life
Music moved her soul
Numbers and music make a whole
Their eyes met in the library
They made sweet noises in the refectory
They soon forgot their books as passion took a hold

July guest – Rosemerry Wahtola Trommer

About Rosemerry Wahtola Trommer

Rosemerry Wahtola Trommer co-hosts Emerging Form (a podcast on creative process), Secret Agents of Change (a surreptitious kindness cabal) and Soul Writer's Circle. Her poetry has appeared on *A Prairie Home Companion*, *PBS News Hour*, *O Magazine*, *American Life in Poetry*, on Carnegie Hall stage, and on river rocks she leaves around town. Her collection *Hush* won the Halcyon Prize. *Naked for Tea* was a finalist for the Able Muse Book Award. Her most recent collection is *All the Honey*. Her daily audio series, *The Poetic Path*, can be found on the Ritual app, her daily poetry practice can be read on her blog, *A*

Hundred Falling Veils, and her book of mindfulness poetry prompts is *Exploring Poetry of Presence II.* One-word mantra: Adjust.

Why I Urge You to Do What You're Passionate About

"And do you know that you're actually going to make more of a difference by focusing on politics than on the culture you're passionate about? You don't know what you might help make happen. Our world is full of the result of unintended as well as intended consequences."
—Yo-Yo Ma, *"Yo-Yo Ma and the Meaning of Life" in The New York Times Magazine, Nov. 20, 2020*

When Rilke travelled through Russia
and studied Saint Francis
and fell in love with the married Salomé.
and wrote poems for *The Book of Hours*,
he could not have known
that over a century later
a woman on another continent
would find herself wrestled by darkness
and find in his poems encouragement
to lean even deeper into darkness
until she could fall in love
with what she feared most.
He could not have known she would
tattoo his words into her memory
and scribe them into her blood
so whenever she walked or lay in the dark
she would have his words ever with her,
and they made her not only more brave
but more wildly alive than she'd been before.
And what if, as his parents had pushed,
Rilke had joined the military
and turned his back on poetry?

And what if he had not gotten himself expelled
from trade school so he could go on
to study literature and art?
What would have become of the woman
a hundred years later
had she not found his poem
and learned from him to love the dark?

Twenty Years Ago, Ten Years Ago, Last Week

If I could go back in time
and offer advice to my younger self,
I wouldn't.
I would let her fail all over again.
I'd let her falter. I'd let her lose.
I'd let her stumble
and struggle and bomb.
But I would lean in close
and let her know
I am deeply in love with her.
It's so easy now to give her this,
this self-compassion in full bloom,
this thing she believed
was impossible.

Thinking of Vincent Painting "Winter"

inspired by the painting "Winter (The Vicarage Garden Under Snow)"
[1] by Vincent Van Gogh and the piano composition "Winter Fields" by
Kayleen Asbo

While he painted the world in browns and grays,
Vincent van Gogh did not yet know
of the throbbing vibrance that would someday
emerge from inside him. He did not yet know
how these somber scenes—like a man alone
shoveling the dim weight of winter—
would give way to an ecstasy of gold,
an elation of blue, rapturous green.
God, I am drawn to these grim, gritty paintings
with their muted schemes and tangled branches,
searching for notes of what will happen—
how he will travel to the warmth of Provence,
will come to share through thick stroke and bright hue
"the terrible passions of humanity."
How he will give everything, everything to his art—
how his talent will grow as the world breaks his heart,
how he will change the way we see beauty,
how he will be wrestled by melancholy.
I imagine him sitting in the bleak Dutch cold,
painting the dreary, dissonant snow,
becoming the painter he's destined to be,
living into the losses, the gifts he does not yet know.

---

1. *https://www.pinterest.com/pin/327425835410102834/*

The Legacy of Gustav Klimt and His Enduring Kiss

After over a hundred years,
the blue flowers in her hair
are still as blue and the ivy
in his hair is still as green
and her face is just as soft
and serene as when she received
the kiss, the kiss that made
the whole world fall in love
with Gustav Klimt. And who
wouldn't want to be caught
forever and ever in a golden
embrace, infinitely tender,
eternally erotic, the way
no kiss truly is? But here
they are, defying the fall,
these lovers, hanging unframed
on the wall of the Belvedere,
still passionate, lust-drowsy,
their love spilling into the halls
as the whole world around
them dissolves into shimmer,
into shine.

No Longer Empty Handed

after the poet pointed out there are dozens of well-known euphemisms for
male masturbation and none for women
How could I not start to think
of circling the black hole,
polishing the pearl,
rubbing the rose bud,
loosening the tight knot,
spreading the soft butter,
frosting the sweet cake,
stirring the soup till it's hot,
dancing on the vortex,
getting sucked into the eddy,
diving into the deep end.
What does it mean
that we don't have language
for a woman who pleases herself?
Consider the tectonic shift,
the solitary wiggle,
the single squirm,
the one-handed time warp,
churning the cream
climbing pink mountain,
traveling to the temple,
spinning the dark silk.
No choking chickens,
no spanking monkeys,
no beating meat,
no wanking.
More like swirling the universe,
mining for diamonds,

finding hidden treasure
wading in the whirlpool,
the reason I can't answer the phone.

August guest – Patty Fletcher

About Patty Fletcher

Patty Fletcher is a single mother with a beautiful daughter, of whom she is enormously proud. She has a great son-in-law and six beautiful grandchildren. From April 2011 through September 2020, she owned and handled a black Labrador from The Seeing Eye® named King Campbell Lee Fletcher A.K.A. Bubba. Sadly, after a long battle with illness on September 24, 2020, King Campbell went to the Rainbow Bridge where all is peace and love. In July 2021, she returned to The Seeing Eye® and was paired with a Black Labrador Golden Retriever cross named Blue.

PATTY'S BLINDNESS...

Patty was born one and a half months premature. Her blindness was caused by her being given too much oxygen in the incubator. She was partially sighted until 1991, at which time she lost her sight due to an infection after cataract surgery and high eye pressure. She used a cane for 31 years before making the change to a guide dog.

WHERE SHE LIVES AND WORKS...

Currently, Patty lives and works in Kingsport, Tenn.

She's the creator and owner of Tell-It-To-The-World Marketing (Author, Blogger, Business Assist), The Writer's Grapevine Online Magazine and the creator and host of the Talk to Tell-It-To-The-World Marketing Podcast.

WRITING GOAL...

Patty writes with the goal of bridging the great chasm which separates the disabled from the non-disabled.

HOBBIES...

Patty's hobbies include reading, music, and attending book clubs via Zoom.

FAVORITE TUNES...

Some of her favorite types of tunes are classic rock, rhythm and blues, and classic country.

FAVORITE READS...

Patty enjoys fantasy, science fiction, and books about the supernatural. She loves books by Stephen King, Dean Koontz, Norah Roberts, and many more. Some favorite books include Norah Roberts' Hide Away, Stephen King's Dark Tower series, J.K. Rowling's Harry Potter series, Robert Jordan's Wheel of Time series, and J.R.R. Tolkien's Lord of the Rings series.

SPIRITUAL FAITH...

Patty describes herself as a spiritual Walker. She says she knows both Mother Goddess and Father God and embraces all they have to offer.

CONTACT...

Email: patty.volunteer1@gmail.com

Find Patty on Smashwords.[1]
Find Patty on Amazon.[2]
Find Patty on Goodreads.[3]
Walk alongside Patty and Chief Seeing Eye® Dog Blue on the Pathway to Freedom.[4]

---

1. https://www.smashwords.com/profile/view/PattyFletcher

2. https://www.amazon.com/Patty-L.-Fletcher/e/B00Q9I7RWG

3. https://www.goodreads.com/author/show/8431191.Patricia_L_Fletcher

4. https://paypal.me/tellittotheworld?locale.x=en_US

Grandfather Tree Speaks

As I walk beside the lake, my time I do take.

I meditate, and share, my happy thoughts by use of the crisp, cold, magical winter air.

Then my rest, I take beneath this loving old tree, who, without complaint shelters me.

My hands I lay upon the bark, my thoughts light, for here there is no dark.

I ask this old Grandfather Tree; "Do you know of my old dear long-gone friend, Grandmother tree?"

His leaves in the wind they do shake, a whispering sound they do make, as he answers me.

I can hear him say, "Yes your Grandmother Tree from long ago I do know and if you listen close to all the leaves, a message from her you are sure to perceive."

And so, I rested silent in the glow of the sunlight, and soon found Grandfather Tree was quite right.

For as the leaves whispered, I did hear from far away, Grandmother Tree say...

"Hello, my friend, I am still here, so never fear.

I have not forgotten you, nor the kindness and love you did give to me."

And so, with that I did rise, giving a contented sigh.

I said to Grandfather Tree, "Thank you kind sir for helping, sheltering, and loving me."

Again, his leaves in the winter wind he did shake, and gave a message for me to take.

"When you partake of the land, do hear, and obey this simple command.

Be wary of the older trees and treat them kindly if you please.

For we are important too, and if you allow, we've much to share with you.

May harmony find you, blessed be."

If Only, for a Moment

They stood, their backs to the world,
safe
Even if only, for a moment
Happy and content
Their arms round each other, her head on his shoulder
His body, strong and lien. Muscles at the ready, hands like a cloud of
thunder
His voice, deep and rich
They move through the house, talking in each room
Stopping in the hall for a kiss
Going onward into the study
There, only a moment
Moving as one to the bed
Tumbling together, in a tangle of hands, arms, and legs
Fire between his fingers, cold, as ice, yet somehow flames on her skin
As they flow together, their passion runs deep
Her mouth on his
Their bodies become one
They melt together in the molten lava of their sex
Their hearts fly
Their passions rise
Her need peeks
His fullness she seeks
Together they explode, the white-hot throbbing, hums low
After, they stand
Their backs to the world
Safe,
if only for a moment

Ever Lost in the Moment

The scorching wind roared angrily across the jagged peaks above. The thundering waves pounded the steep cliffs below.

Standing, their bare toes clinging to the rocks, naked in the fading day. Faces moist with the ocean spray. The sunset a ball of fiery molten liquid melting into the churning sea.

He, seeing her there, dangerously close to the edge. She, breathing the dank salty air. Her ebony hair streaming long and beautiful round her there.

He, drinking her in, his senses catching fire with want and desire. She, like a deer, sensing danger in the wind, felt him there.

Turning to him, her mouth parting in a gorgeous smile, they stood, the only sound the roaring of the wind, pounding of the waves, and song of the gulls. Their hearts beat as one. In perfect time with the rhythmic sea, they knew, they would be, ever lost in the moment.

September guest – Yvette Prior

About Yvette Prior

Yvette Prior lives on the East Coast of the United States with her spouse, Chris, and together they have three adult children, two grandchildren, and no pets (after having many dogs over the years).

Yvette enjoys working with people and her varied work background includes education, social work, hospitality management, and lots of outreach. Her passion area is studying about health and wellness and after earning a Ph.D. in I-O Psychology, she poured into waiting book projects and she has not stopped writing since.

Her goal as a writer is to educate, edify, and encourage readers. Her personal blog can be found at priorhouse.wordpress.com

Dancing with Angst

Feeling angst
familiar stance
like a close friend
mixed amends
While it comes and goes
my angst
is not merely woes
Oh no...
No, indeed
because dancing with angst
plants seeds
removes weeds
reaping and sowing
learning and growing
We dance with angst
for many reasons
not just seeding and weeding
Also for cleaning and weaning
aerating
freeing
uplifting self and others
Steadying
Loving deeper
Serving
Promise keeper
When we embrace our angst
like a dance
we have flexibility and ease
stiffness leaves
Angst in morning's sorrow

managed and felt
Sometimes tucked away
until tomorrow
Knowing dawn will eventually melt
heaviness and fray
hope emerges
with each new day
Angst is more than parching toil
It is compost enriching the soil
Filling one up inside
Keeping a humble stride
Broken wings might not fly
but we can glide
we can slide
We adjust our ride
Because in God,
we fully abide
Dancing with angst
is part of the deal
As wings heal
It keeps us real
Angst can be pain
...a setback
Angst can bring humility
...a dish of humble pie
Angst can be off and on
like rain after the sun
nothing is by chance
this is why we dance
with our angst
God appointments
detours assigned

humans refined
one season at a time
Did angst weigh heavy today?
Get up and dance, is what I say
Each coda starts with a plié
Adjust your stay
arranging, quieting, maintaining
adapting along the way
Poised energy with angst
embracing circumstance
two feet, back on the ground
stability has different sounds
Staying stable
through highs and lows
strengthens one like steel
because humans heal
we strategize
then fortify
staying even keeled
moving from toes to heels
I softly smile
Ready for the next mile
Angst is more than only woe
even though we are glad to see it go
it can magnify our joy
changement can stir up appreciation
you cannot fully know
how dancing with angst helps you grow
until you have been cut down
pounded out, unwound
After the angst
filled to the brim

inner light no longer dim
Elevated after being frustrated
Fortified from trial
Inner peace, genuine smile
Angst gone, new song
Essence returned
Lessons learned
I am more than okay
I am fully breathing
Rather than seething
I choose forgiveness
Rather than counting losses
I choose understanding
Rather than counting thorns
I choose love
I choose a smile and confidence posture
as I face each season
I have many reasons
to dance with my angst
It is so good to be alive
angst helps me thrive
Angst is not a permanent ride
But an essential part of life's tide

Dancing in circumstance
Praying with endurance
when angst eases or leaves
Humility is in the breeze
Does my angst
keep pride at bay?
Stop my head from swelling?
There is no telling
all the reasons
for life's dance
with angst
It is not by chance
When angst and I dance
Smooth groove, side to side
bumpy, beautiful stride
Angst lets me enhance
Develop my balance
put discouragement at bay
Learning each day
To embrace the sway

Picture credit: Tulip by Yvette Prior

Quiet Fuel of Passion

If you choose to live life
with choices based on passion
And not merely for money
not power
Not what the world
says is "in" for this hour
If you choose to live life
laden with meaning
it can your heart
fully beating
passion can quietly fuel you
Soothe you
Help you navigate with meaning
because values
are always screaming
beneath the scenes
often quietly
and unheard
Yet they steer the way
impacting the choices we make
every single day
To be fueled from passion

      one must separate
      values from goals
      so you can understand
      what makes you go
      we don't always know
      as it lies low
      quietly

behind the screen
Invisible
Guiding machine

To value making a difference
It changes your approach
Thinking of others
faith, beyond reproach
Heavenly rewards
impacts choices
while the heart rejoices
Living passionately
with values guiding
changes how we respond
prevents colliding
filters how we process outcomes
Not keeping track of certain sums
Values determine
how we manage change

    or endure lack of variety

how we stay stable

    or augment feeling stuck

how we manage options

    or accept few choices

In times of great hardship
Does passion leak?
Do we go from strong to weak?
No, there can strength in weakness.

Recover as needed.
Heal from trials.
Restoration
Trusting God all the while
As things can work FOR good.
Even though it does not feel great
to deflate

    suffer
    wait

There is interplay
with joy and struggle
When passion fuels behind the scenes
It makes struggles worth it
A necessary means
When there is meaning in what we do
we fail forward
We don't become lower
Instead, we cope to ascend
Carrying burdens
Like helpful friends
When we choose
to make a difference
it makes trials worthwhile
laden with meaning
fully breathing

Picture credit: Coffee mug by Yvette Prior

"We are a Bird," he said

The question on date night:
What animal describes your partnership?
"We are a Bird," said He
A Bird?
Was this really what I heard?
Is that even an animal?
Yes.
"We are a Bird," said He
So we began to break it down.
The idea took flight

> and the bird
> it fit our life
> kinda right

Bird art around the house
ceramic pair

from the 20th year
while enjoying Plan C
Three metal birds
from early Florida years
A symbol of many joys
and a handful of tears
"We are a Bird," said He
Because of the real birds, too

> our comrades in the yard
> reminding us to lighten up
> when life felt hard

Those special birds
that led to the Avian Friends book
It was an unexpected hook
To have such special words
inspired by backyard birds
as they soothed a grieving heart
Love and hope they did impart
Indeed, there was a bird theme
A meme
this trend
our feathered friends
And how we helped each other mend
Partnership dividend

feel so free
no oppression
cultivating harmony

Birds reminded us of God's provisions
Whether needs were large or small
Because as He cares for the smallest sparrow
His wings cover us all
His love fills our essence
The gift of in-dwelling presence
"We are a Bird," said He
Because you let me breathe

my partner, lover, friend
you helped me ascend
nudged me to soar
let me glide so free
ample solitude
this life of "we"

Our decades of togetherness

    co-parenting
    colleague
    problem solver
    passionate friend
    confidant
    my other half
    a Godsend

You and me....
sharing our wings
with all that life brings
And our nest?
What of our nest?

    safety
    companionship
    conversation
    humbleness
    soothing rest
    sleep
    dream
    heal
    play
    create
    feed
    breed

    The nest is also for outreach

perch point so fine
A nest with opened shutters

is simple and sublime

Filled up
to help others too
margins
leaving room
to give and serve
with time to nestle in
preserve, fill back to the rim

"We are a Bird," said He
My heart fluttered!
like feathers on a flapping wing
Because for almost thirty years
He, has made my heart sing
I smiled and my eyes grew wet
Because we aren't even done yet
there is more time to live
more time to give
more time of tenderness
togetherness
in
and out
of our enjoyable little nest

Picture caption: Two birds by Yvette Prior

Poetic Sleep

After a long writing week
words began to seep
Right into my sleep
A passion for poetry
Poured over me
Tossing and turning
Lines were churning

    cognitive forming
    iambic storming

Waking to see the time
I had yet another rhyme
Wanting to get up

    and write words down
    but sleep mattered more
    Would not back down
    exhausted
    worn to the core

In and out of wakefulness
I had feelings of gratefulness

    trickles of happiness
    as the poetry flowed
    In a rhyming sleep show

How fun was the week-long writing mode
where ideas were churned from the soul

and then came this night
the poetry faucet gushing
So waking with morning coffee
I did a little rushing
to get a pen and notebook
to start drafting in my nook

But for goodness sake
now that I was wide awake

    ideas were quieted
    the poems that were there
    all night long
    whispering like a song
    were now...
    simply gone

All those words
I faintly heard
Were now gone
it was quite absurd
It was not fair
Rhymes were churning
while tossing and turning
But now sitting in my armchair
Nothing was oozing
The words I heard
Were now off snoozing -

    rhyme schemes were asleep
    I almost wanted to weep

Sipping coffee

staring at blank sheets
I smiled to think of the amazing poetic sleep

Picture credit: Water by Yvette Prior

October guest – Judy Mastrangelo

About Judy Mastrangelo

Judy Mastrangelo has written and illustrated several books, which include themes of Poetry, Fairytales, and Fairies. She follows in the tradition of "The Art of the Golden Age of Illustration". Some of her titles include: a series of four Fairy books: "Portal to the Land of Fae" which include Flower Fairies, Fairy Tale Fairies, Secrets of the Fairies, and Mystical Fairies. Additional books include "What Do Bunnies Do All Day?", "Enchanted Fairy Tales", which she illustrated and adapted, "The Star", illustrating the poem Twinkle, Twinkle Little Star, and her new fairy tale "The Magic Blanket". Besides creating books, her artwork has been used in several Inspirational Oracle Card Decks, as well as some that she has also written herself. She licenses her artwork for many products, including Art Prints and Wall Murals. Judy has taught Creative Drama and Dance as well as Painting, to Children and Adults, and has directed her own Community Theater for all ages. As part of her work, she enjoys encouraging people to develop their own Imagination and Artistic Talents.

You can visit her at www.judymastrangelo.com[1]

---

1. http://www.judymastrangelo.com

Gaia's Love

Gaia's Love permeates throughout.
Her deep passion for every water droplet,
leaf, flower, butterfly, frog, and snail, can be seen and felt.
Breathe deeply of the Air surrounding her.
She appears out of Purple Sunset, Sunrise Clouds.
She can be seen reflected in ripping waters,
rising from her earthly hills and mountains,
as graceful leaves, rainbows,
and flowers bedeck her.
Her Tree Spirits shelter, protecting and adorning
glorious Nature with Beloved Birds, and Dragonflies.
All in the Human World Love her too.

Picture Credit: "Gaia" painting by Judy Mastrangelo

The Fairy Path

Follow me down the Fairy Path to visit
Enchanting Magical Worlds
you've only seen or felt
in Dreams.
You will return refreshed and rejuvenated,
full of Life, Love,
and Passion for Being.

Picture Credit: "The Fairy Path" painting by Judy Mastrangelo

Pan and Unicorn

The God Pan pipes his Magical Melodies
deep in a Secret Forest.
Both he and his Unicorn companion are poised,
waiting to hear an answering song.

Who will respond to the call?
Perhaps the sweet voice of a Wood Nymph,
the singing of a Graceful Sylph,
or just the lyrical melody of a Lark.

Picture Credit: "Pan and Unicorn" painting by Judy Mastrangelo

Garden of the Sun and Moon

They say that as the Lady Moon
gracefully touches the trees,
after floating in the sky all night,
she comes to a special place.
It is here that she meets her Soul Mate the Sun,
as he prepares to rise and light the Earth by day.
The time they are together may seem
but an instant to you or me,
but they experience it as many blissful hours.
And so the Sun and Moon
embrace in their Secret Love Garden.
They are unseen by all but the gentle Deer,
in the Twilight of Clouds and Roses.

Picture Credit: "Garden Of The Sun And Moon" painting by Judy Mastrangelo

Moonlight Fairy

A Fairy tends her dewdrops by Moonlight.
Breathless and Hopeful,
waiting for Love that will quiver her Heart.
She adores her Beloved from afar.
Wanting, Yearning,

Hoping they will soon caress.
She sees him in her Dream State,
and Sings out.
Soon ~ from the mist,
he coalesces.
Sparkling, shimmering,
a Handsome Being.
Far beyond her wildest imagination!
Soon they meld in gentle embrace.

Picture Credit: "Moonlight Fairy" painting by Judy Mastrangelo

Fairy Wedding

The Fairy King and Queen gaze adoringly, wide eyed, bright eyed, in
the Twilight,
holding each other, feeling the warmth.
Gently touching hands, sensing vibrations running through their
graceful bodies,
gazing lovingly in Evening Sunset,
framed by Moon and Stars.
Their Joyful retinue of Fairies dance happily
to lilting Music, through the Air and Trees,
twirling Flower Garlands
in evening Palace Gardens.
The Midnight Magic reaches culmination
as our Regal Couple are escorted to their
sumptuous Wedding Chamber,
bedecked with sweetly scented
Magnolia and Rose petals.
Parting open gossamer translucent curtains
to reveal a bed of blossoms.
Sinking softly, sweetly, dancing,
they are watched over by
fluttering lightning fire flies,
blinking golden light
upon their awestruck lovely souls.

Picture Credit: "Fairy Wedding" painting by Judy Mastrangelo

November guest – Penny Wilson

About Penny Wilson

Penny Wilson is a freelance writer who writes in several genres. A love of reading was instilled in her at an early age. This led to her reading well above her grade level as a child. Because of this, her love of poetry and writing has been life-long.

She has written articles for WOW Women on Writing. Her poetry has been published in online journals, such as Ariel Chart, Spill Words Press and the Poppy Road Review. Penny is a member of the Austin Poetry Society. Her poetry has been featured in the publication America's Emerging Poets 2018 & 2019 by Z Publishing and Poets Quarterly and Dual Coast Magazine published by Prolific Press.

Penny is an advocate for Mental Health Awareness and has the page "Mental Health Help" on her blog. She writes about the struggles of mental illnesses and Depression. She is passionate about spreading awareness for Suicide Prevention and Domestic Abuse. She expresses her passion through her writings of poetry and life experiences. You can find more of her writings on her blog at https://pennywilsonwrites.com/ and follow her on Twitter @pennywilson123.

What Remains

Heaven
in your arms
Utopia
in those eyes
Days
in Paradise
Nights
in Bliss
My soul,
A small price to pay
What remains?
Hell.

Something Worth Losing

I've never had anything
of real value
Just a few trinkets
I've no palatial dwelling
no shiny chariot
I have no gold or silver
to barter with
My meals are
simple fair
My riches have amounted to
the warmth of the sun
chasing away the chills
the earth prosperous and abundant
with life all around me
I have water enough
to quench these lips
and nourish my garden
All that I require
is provided me
But, you...
Having you
gave me something
worth losing

The Penalty

My mind's eye
still holds you
in an embrace
I knew there

would be a price
A penalty,
for loving you
I didn't know,
how long
that penalty would last
A lifetime,
my beloved
and beyond

The Price Paid

I learned of
broken wings
and broken dreams
the human
touch
most coveted
left deepest
of scars
when I write
my muse whispers
of yesterdays
my heart
deciphering
the path unearthed
the price
paid
for love

Love Felt

to know
your heart skips a beat
to be
the whisper
on
the tip of your tongue
I see the glimmer
in your eyes
and hear
the catch
in your breath
souls
touching
this
this is
more than physical
this
is love
felt

A Whispered name

The breeze brings the
fragrance of wildflowers
and your skin
your touch
a whisper
your caress
my desire
your desire
inflames me
share with me
your longing
bring to me
your hand and heart
speak my name
that I may whisper
yours

A Splash of Heaven

Splash me with the blue
of heaven
The exact color of
Your eyes
Let me flow
between your fingers
Quell my parched
Skin
Touch
Me
Leaving my Eden
Quenched
Yearning only
another splash
of Heaven

Special guest – Colleen Chesebro

I invited Colleen Chesebro to be my special guest for this edition of Poetry Treasures. My December 2022 Treasuring Poetry article was dedicated to the late Sue Vincent, a talented poet, writer, and a good friend.

Colleen recently published a new poetry collection called "Fairies, Myths, & Magic II—A Winter Celebration" which featured a delightful poem, "Swift Passage", dedicated to Sue Vincent. Colleen has graciously included that beautiful poem in her contributions to this anthology.

About Colleen Chesebro

Colleen M. Chesebro grew up in a large city in the Midwest. Keen on making her own way in the world, she joined the United States Air Force after graduation to tour the world and find herself. To this day, that search continues.

An avid reader, Chesebro rekindled her love of writing poetry after years spent working in the accounting industry. These days, she loves crafting syllabic poetry, flash fiction, creative fiction and nonfiction.

In addition to poetry books, Chesebro's publishing career includes participation in various anthologies featuring short stories, flash fiction, and poetry. She's an avid supporter of her writing community on Word Craft Poetry.com by sponsoring a weekly syllabic poetry challenge, called #TankaTuesday, where participants experiment with traditional and current forms of Japanese and American syllabic poetry. Chesebro is an assistant editor of The Congress of the Rough Writers Flash Fiction Anthology & Gitty Up Press, a micro-press founded by Charli Mills and Carrot Ranch.com.

In January 2022, Colleen founded Unicorn Cats Publishing Services to assist poets and authors in creating eBooks and print books for publication. In addition, she creates affordable book covers for Kindle and print books.

Chesebro lives in the house of her dreams in mid-Michigan, surrounded by the Great Lakes with her husband and two (unicorn) cats, Chloe & Sophie.

Swift Passage

sunlight, a pink aurora in the shining sky,
from the brushwood, the crows take wing
shadows dance and small birds sing,
swift passage comes for ancestral souls on high,
faery queens gather to welcome their otherworldly kin
she who walked among those bound to the earth
now takes passage within the Bardo of her rebirth,
spring rain washes away the pain of our loss and chagrin,
raise your arm to the circle of the sun
close your eyes and breathe, Inhale the celestial breath
thank you for the golden words of wisdom you've spun
your earthly quest is won

"Swift Passage" first appeared in "Fairies, Myths, & Magic II—A Winter Celebration" (Dedicated to my friend, Sue Vincent 1958-2021)

The Lady Waits, chōka

a covert meeting—
she stays for her one truelove
fiery passions burn
wintery winds rough bluster
does naught to cure sin,
her seas wild, countenance calm
a constant struggle
his abandoned possession...
she waits for his attention

Gray – Winter's Passion

The gray sky bleeds raindrops into my world.
January feels leaden, a Michigan-gray,
displaying a perpetual pallor that cloaks
the woods near my home in a silvery mist.
Even the pine trees wear greenish-gray shrouds,
dark phantom smudges against the gray sky.
Winter and its frosty brightness have abandoned me.
Gone are the nights when snow-light
played on the ceiling above the curtains,
closed—to shut out the glare of the streetlight.
Instead, gray shadows flirt in the darkness.
This gray is unresponsive, unattached, and neutral...
it won't be the star of the show, the vibrant leader, or the director.
The final moment of winter's passion has passed.
This color is too safe and weak for that.
Yet, this gray of winter lightens me
from living in a riotous world.
Everything I do is stitched with its color—
shades of gray saturate—like whispers in the corners,
where light and sound can't penetrate.
Gray is an old soul searching for the light.

Passion Play

Discover your passion...
change your perspective
accept an outlook for immense happiness
be open to first times
find your adventure
Are you ready to change?
...to know your passion?
remember—life happens for you, not to you,
listen to the silence
the answers are there
Tap into your desires—
what is it you love?
nourish your mind to recognize your own strengths
face your fears, don't hold back
embrace your passion!

Love's Reply

First light begins the day; shadows recede in moon glow.
A pale gauze of clouds stretches tight against a blue sky.
Streets wet with melting snow echo when cars slow.
A rabbit pierces the crusty glaze, long distance tracks pass by.

In the darkness, we embrace our soul's collective power.
Together, each half of us makes a whole, our life complete.
You're a wild February snowstorm, and I'm a soft April shower.
Together, our love grows velvet like a rose, pure and sweet.

The silent gray of dusk descends; a setting sun pinks the sky.
Canadian geese take wing, songs of adventure voiced in the night.
We settle in front of the fireplace, mesmerized by the flames last goodbye.
Darkness comes on cat feet, stealthy—stealing the light.

Youth slips from my face; the lines in the mirror magnify the past.
Death comes early in my family; I calculate the time ahead.
Will the years catch up to the two of us? Can we make the time last?
The ticking of the clock sounds loud in the shadowy places in my head.

It's another year around the sun. Time slows down, our hearts leap.
We can almost touch the stars as dawn's golden fire kisses the sky,
while all around us, the rest of the world sleeps, silent and deep.
After all these years, it's still us—forever entwined, love's reply.
this moment...
the darkness before dawn
spent with you

Green Fire Woman

the full moon...
I memorize the night
you left me
Dreams like star-smoke haunt the velvet night,
ancient trees sway and dance in the wind.
I recall the sounds—the chanting of spells,
cast to air, earth, fire, and water.
Breathe in the universe's sky rhythm,
the sound of blood rushing through my veins,
as a gauze of morning clouds embraced
the passion of a green fire woman.
falling stars
burnish the night sky
tears in my eyes

Special guest – D. Wallace Peach

About D. Wallace Peach

Best-selling fantasy author D. Wallace Peach indulges her imagination in the world of words. She's published twenty fantasy novels and participated in anthologies featuring short stories, flash fiction, and poetry. An avid supporter of the arts, she's produced annual anthologies of Oregon prose, poetry, and photography.

Words

I conjure you from the airy cauldron
Of a waltzing barn-swallow sky
From drowned groves and spring-fed seas
Rocks where speckled salamanders hide
You beckon from the valleys of a juniper moon
Sketched visions with night's silver frost
Sweet and bitter the taste of your kisses
Moody ballads strummed to my heart's pulse
You are stubborn and eager, my wily lovers
Mummers in a bonfire's fairy light
Slipping between the evergreen
The chase begun
A torturous teasing
I cannot live without

The Mermaid

weave into my dreams
watery visions of pearls
even as I drown
let me drift with the fishes
charmed by your silvery tail

Keep it Tight

We crowd the kitchen
Keeping it loose while whipping up a medley
Reeling to a rainbow ballad
From sink to fridge and back again
A dosey-doe of our heart's rhythm
Until the inevitable collision
Spilled wine, grabby hands
A split-second kiss and spin
We hang tight, seen it all before
Through the years
But it never grows old
(Inspired by: Lee, Amos. "Keep it Loose, Keep it Tight." *Amos Lee.*
Blue Note Records, 2005)

Timeless

In the hushed slumber of dawn
When light threads her lavender loom
Through groves stirring with doves
You exhale a soft savannah sigh
A languid caress of gray feathers
Beneath the patter on a tin roof
In our northern rainforest room
I curl against arthritic shoulders
The flame of your skin burning
An eternity of winters to ash
I surrender to timeless beauty
Beholding the illusion of youth
Woven through your silver hair

About the Publisher

WordCrafter Press publishes quality books and anthologies. Learn more about *WordCrafter* and keep updated on current online book events, writing contests, up coming book blog tours and new releases on the *Writing to be Read* authors' blog: https://writingtoberead.com/